MEDITATIONS

WITH THOMAS BERRY

With additional material by Brian Swimme

Selected by June Raymond

Independent Publishing Platform
GreenSpirit Book Series, 2021
www.greenspirit.org.uk
GreenSpirit is a registered charity based in the UK. The main contents/written
material, editing, design and promotional work for its books is done on a purely
voluntary basis or given freely by contributors who share a passion for
Gaia-centred spirituality.

ISBN: 9798753834591 (hardback) / 9798454067786 (paperback)

Introduction © June Raymond
First published by GreenSpirit Books in 2010.
A low-cost eBook edition of *GreenSpirit Reflections* is also available.

Quotations by permission of Brian Swimme
and the Estate of the late Thomas Berry.

Design and artwork by Stephen Wollaston (Santoshan)
Photograph of St Francis statue courtesy of Marty Ostrow

Images with copyright:
Page 15 © Serg64/Shutterstock.com
Page 64 © Sergey Nivens/Shutterstock.com
Page 92 © Evdokimov Maxim/Shutterstock.com

MEDITATIONS

WITH THOMAS BERRY

These meditations are dedicated with love

to our beautiful planet.

Contents

Introduction

Thomas Berry 1914-2009

When Thomas Berry was eleven years old his parents moved to the country and he had an experience which was to stay with him all his life. He wandered down to a creek and saw beyond it a meadow covered in white lilies rising above thick grass. There were crickets singing and woodlands in the distance and clouds in a clear sky. The effects of this moment, he said, lay behind all his philosophy and religious awareness. When he was twenty he became a Passionist priest and later an academic specialising in cultural history. However, the fundamental direction of his life remained his commitment to the environment as the primary manifestation of the divine and to the need to prevent its destruction.

Berry developed a profound knowledge of Asian thought and was much influenced by the Asian scholar, Theodore de Bary of Columbia University. He also learnt from Teilhard de Chardin who had seen the world as one in which spirituality was not the province of the human alone but something which from the beginning had pervaded the whole. For Berry the well-being of the Earth was fundamental and he suggested that we should go to creation as the primary revelation and our primary connection with the divine. In 1970 he founded the Riverdale Center of Religious Research in Riverdale, New York, a base from which he further developed his thinking on human-Earth relationships.

Berry believed that we are on the cusp of a new way of being on our planet. Our present era is the Cenozoic, the last 65 million years in which the creativity of the Earth blossomed, leading to the coming of humanity. But as we have taken over Earth's ecology we have been responsible for such environmental destruction that this Cenozoic era is coming to an end. The next era Berry believed is the Ecozoic, in which the future of the Earth will depend on our having a completely different relationship with it. Instead of our influence being one of exploitation and destruction, it is to be one of an 'integral participation' with all other members of our planetary community. He found in indigenous peoples such as Native Americans something of the spiritual communion with all beings that he saw as essential.

Unlike some modern thinkers, Berry did not regard humanity as a mistake the universe has made but as an important part of the whole. He understood that as the universe unfolds it follows three fundamental tendencies: differentiation, subjectivity or inner awareness, and ever deepening communion. In humanity these processes reached a moment in which the universe became aware of itself and its own beauty.

But the human race has become fragmented and divorced from its true relationship with creation and Berry believed we need a new story, one that would unite human beings instead of dividing them and would restore us to our place in the cosmos rather than separating us from it. This new unifying story is that of the cosmos itself. In 1992 he published *The Universe Story* with cosmologist Brian Swimme. They drew on contemporary scientific knowledge to trace the story 'from the primordial flaring forth to the Ecozoic era' in what they describe as 'a celebration of the unfolding cosmos'.

Thomas Berry also had very practical ideas about how we might avert global catastrophe and begin the process of restoring human society to its rightful place in the cosmic community. If we are able to replace a narrow human perspective with a recognition that our wellbeing is dependent on the wellbeing of the whole Earth community, every branch of learning can be transformed. Berry considered economics to be particularly dysfunctional; the Earth is our primary capital and when we plunder it we too are in deficit. However he reserved his sternest criticism for the two institutions which he considered had most responsibility; the churches and the universities. Both he saw as aggravating the problem, teaching and encouraging people to exploit the natural world. Other areas which he considered needed reinventing were law, medicine and technology.

Berry felt that it is difficult for us to change our ways as we have become paralysed by a destructive, addictive and pathological lifestyle. He was nevertheless an optimist. Looking at the history of the cosmos and understanding the divine essence we share with creation, he believed that we can go forward as a positive part of Earth's unfolding and fulfilment.

A suggested way of using these meditations

You can obviously use the book in any way that suits you, however for those who find it helpful here is a suggested way of meditating.

Find a quiet place where you will not be disturbed. You may like to choose a spot which looks out onto the world outside. Some people light a candle. Sit in a comfortable chair with a straight back and both feet on the ground, otherwise as relaxed and peaceful as possible. Now look at the place you are in, both in the room and what is going on outside. Spend time on this but try simply to observe where you are without making any judgements.

Close your eyes and become aware of every sound, again both inside and outside your room. Finally notice your own body and how it feels. If you find anything distracting notice but don't try to change it, just be aware and then let go.

Now go back to your sense of the place you are in. This is a vibrant moment of creation, everything filled with life down to the vibrating of atoms. This moment and this space are a sacred manifestation of Earth's life. It is dependent on all that has gone before, to create it and all else that is, to hold it in being. You are part of it, not an alien, but intrinsic to the whole. Stay with an awareness of being held in this moment by all that is.

Now go to the meditations and slowly read a single page. Stay with any words or ideas that speak to you. Give yourself time to feel your way in to understanding and exploring this awareness until you become part of the cosmos knowing itself.

At the end of your meditation send your thanksgiving and blessing back to the universe and especially to our own Earth.

~ JUNE RAYMOND

Publisher's Note:

The reader will notice that throughout the text the word 'Earth' is sometimes capitalized and sometimes not. This is because Thomas Berry's work was published by several different publishers whose styles differed. We have retained the original styling in all cases.

A number of the quotations in this book are from *The Universe Story* which Thomas Berry jointly authored with Brian Swimme. Please note that many of these, particularly those in Chapter 1, would originally have been contributed by Brian.

Creation's Beauty
and Violence

1

All the energy that would ever

exist in the entire course of time

erupted in a single quantum.

If in the future stars would blaze

and lizards would blink in their light,

these actions would be

powered by the same numinous

energy that flared forth at the

dawn of time.

There was no place in the
universe that was separate from
the originating power of the universe.

Even space-time itself was a tossing,
churning, foaming out of the
originating reality instant
by instant.

The realm or power that brings forth the universe

is not itself an event in time, nor a position in space,

but is rather the very matrix out of which the

conditions arise that enable temporal events

to occur in space.

Though the originating power gave birth to

the universe fifteen billion years ago,

this realm of power is not simply located there

at that point of time,

but is rather a condition of every moment of

the universe, past, present,

and to come.

The vitality of a dolphin as it

squiggles high in the summer

sun…is directly dependent upon

the elegance of the dynamics at

the beginning of time.

The story of the universe is a
story of majesty and beauty as
well as of violence and disruption,
a drama filled with both
elegance and ruin.

The Universe thrives on
the edge of a knife.

If it increased its strength of
expansion it would blow up;
if it decreased its strength of
expansion it would collapse.

By holding itself on the edge it
enables great beauty to unfold.

Every existence is a mode of

divine presence.

Beauty, elegance, and destruction are
all layered into our ancestral origin.

Our birth required drastic and
vehement disruption of
well-ordered communities of beings.

Both infinitely patient,
slow processes and sudden,
cosmic intensifications are
required to carry the universe
through the unfurling of
its material-psychic adventure.

Violence and destruction are

dimensions of the universe.

They are present at every level of

existence: the elemental,

the geological, the organic,

the human.

Humans give voice to their most

exalted and terrible feelings only

because they find themselves

immersed in the universe filled

with such awesome realities.

Only by dealing with the difficulty
does the creativity come forth.

The violence associated with the
hawk starving to death or the vole
being consumed are intrinsically tied to
the creativity of each.

The beauty of their response
arises from an inherently
difficult situation.

Only because expansion met the obstacle of

gravitation did the galaxies come forth.

In a similar way the wings of the birds

and the musculature of the elephants

arose out of the careful embrace

of the negative or obstructing aspects

of the gravitational attraction.

Any life forms that might awake in a world

without gravity's hindrances to motion would be

incapable of inventing the anatomy

of the cheetah.

Great art, monumental speculative philosophy,

profound institutional and social reform,

epochal works of music,

and world-transforming technical inventions

have been created by individuals stunned by

suffering and violence.

To eliminate the tension would be

to eliminate the beauty.

Perhaps the only word to describe

the world that gave birth to

the human form of life is paradise.

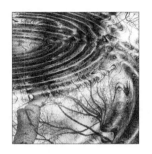

Diversity

2

In the universe,

to be

is to be different.

The mystery that lies behind

the void must have

an awesome imagination;

it must have an amazing capacity

to dream in order to

come up with such an

extraordinary self-manifestation.

Nature abhors uniformity.

Nature not only produces
species diversity
but also individual diversity.
Nature produces individuals.

No two days are the same,
no two snowflakes, no two flowers, trees,
or any other of the infinite life-forms.

There is an awe and reverence

due to the stars in the heavens,

the sun, and all heavenly bodies;

to the seas and the continents;

to all living forms of trees and flowers;

to the myriad expressions of life in the sea;

to the animals of the forests

and the birds of the air.

To wantonly destroy a living species

is to silence forever a divine voice.

We now live not so much in

a *cosmos* as in a *cosmogenesis*;

that is, a universe ever coming

into being through an irreversible

sequence of transformations moving,

in the larger arc of its development,

from a lesser to a greater order of

complexity and from a lesser to

great consciousness.

Interiority

3

There is a Christ dimension of the

universe from the beginning.

There is, from its origin,

a pervasive, numinous,

guiding mystery in the universe

that is designated by different names

in different traditions.

The universe carries within itself

a psychic-spiritual as well as a

physical-material dimension.

Otherwise human consciousness

emerges out of nowhere.

The human activates the most

profound dimension of the universe itself,

its capacity to reflect on and celebrate

itself in conscious self-awareness.

Every being has its own interior,

its self, its mystery,

its numinous aspect.

All things in the universe,

in their subjectivity,

are pervaded by

inherent tendencies toward

fulfilment of their potential.

There is a spiritual capacity in

carbon as there is a carbon

component functioning in our

highest spiritual experience.

If some scientists consider that all

this is a merely material process,

then what they call matter,

I call mind, soul, spirit

or consciousness.

To speak of a Milky Way that does not have
inherent powers to recombine into a
form capable of inner feelings
is to speak of an abstract Milky Way,
one that has no existence in reality.

In this universe the Milky Way expresses its
inner depth in Emily Dickinson's poetry,
for Emily Dickinson is a dimension of
the galaxy's development...

Emily Dickinson in her person
and in her poetry activates an
inner dimension of the Milky Way.

Poetry and the depth of soul

emerge from the human world

because the inner form of the

mountains and the numinous

quality of the sky have activated

these depths in the human.

The human being within the
universe is a sounding board
within a musical instrument.

Our mathematics and our poetry
are the merest echoes of the
universe entire.

Walt Whitman is a space the

milky way fashioned

to feel its own grandeur.

Community

4

Everything in the universe is

genetically cousin to

everything else.

There is literally one family,

one bonding, in the universe,

because everything is descended from

the same source.

Nothing is completely itself

without everything else.

The natural world is the larger
sacred community to which
we belong.

To become alienated from this
community is to become destitute
in all that makes us human.

To damage this community is to
diminish our own existence.

The universe is a communion and

a community.

We ourselves are that communion

become conscious of itself.

Gravitation…binds everything
together so closely that nothing
can ever be separated from
everything else.

Alienation is an impossibility.

We can *feel* alienated,
but we can never *be* alienated.

Any being can benefit only if the

larger context of its existence benefits.

This law can be seen in

the honey bee and the flower.

Both benefit when the bee comes

to drink the nectar of the flower:

the flower is fertilised,

the bee obtains what it needs

for making its honey.

The tree is nourished by the soil;

the tree nourishes the soil

with its leaves.

It is the ancient law of reciprocity.

Whoever gives must also receive.

The face of the bear, the size of her arm,

the structure of her eyes,

the thickness of her fur – these are dimensions

of her temperate forest community.

The bear herself is

meaningless outside this enveloping

web of relations.

The subjectivity of a dragonfly
cannot be simplistically separated
from the objectivity of its pond
– the pond's very shape was
decisive in shaping the
dragonfly's mind.

There is no such thing as 'human community'

without the earth and the soil and

the air and the water

and all living forms.

Humans are woven into this

larger community.

The large community is the

sacred community.

To be Human

5

We bear the universe in our
beings as the universe bears us
in its being.

The two have a total presence to
each other and to that deeper
mystery out of which both
the universe and ourselves
have emerged.

The human is that being in whom
the universe reflects on and
celebrates itself.

It is not that we think the universe;
the universe rather
thinks *itself*, in us
and through us.

The human is neither an
addendum nor an intrusion into
the universe.

We are quintessentially integral
with the universe.

We need to experience the divine revelation

presented to us in the natural world.

The psalms do indeed tell us that

the mountains and the birds praise God.

But do we have to read the Scriptures

to experience that?

Our human responsibility as one voice among

so many throughout the universe is to

develop our capacities to listen as

incessantly as the hovering hydrogen atoms,

as profoundly as our primal ancestors

and their faithful descendants in

today's indigenous peoples.

The adventure of the universe depends on

our capacity to listen.

Why do we have such a wonderful sense of God?
Because we live in such a gorgeous world.

We wonder at the magnificence of whatever it is
that brought the world into being.
This leads to a sense of adoration.

We have a sense of immense gratitude
that we participate in such a beautiful world.
This adoration, this gratitude, we call religion.

Now, however, as our outer world is diminished,
our inner world is dried up.

The greatest of human discoveries

in the future will be the discovery

of human intimacy with all those

other modes of being that live

with us on this planet,

inspire our art and literature

reveal that numinous world

whence all things come into being,

and with which we exchange the

very substance of life.

Human Destruction

6

The industrial age itself...can be
described as a period of
technological entrancement,
an altered state of consciousness,
a mental fixation that alone can
explain how we came to ruin our
air and water and soil and to
severely damage our basic life
systems under the illusion that
this was 'progress.'

Undisciplined expansion and self-inflation
lead only to destruction.

Apart from the well-being of the
earth no subordinate life system
can survive.

We are losing splendid and
intimate modes of divine presence.
We are, perhaps, losing ourselves.

To designate human plundering of

the planet as 'progress' is an

unbearable distortion.

Yet that is precisely what we

have been doing.

We are not talking to the river,

we are not listening to the river.

We have broken the great conversation.

By breaking the conversation,

we have shattered

the universe.

The human is derivative,

the earth is primary.

The most absurd thing for us to

believe is that we can have an

expanding human economy with a

diminishing earth economy.

What happens to the nonhuman
happens to the human.

If the outer world is diminished in
its grandeur then the emotional,
imaginative, intellectual and
spiritual life of the human is
diminished or extinguished.

We cannot make a blade of grass,
but there is liable not to be a blade
of grass if we do not accept it,
protect it, and foster it.

Without the soaring birds,

the great forests, the sounds and

colouration of the insects,

the free-flowing streams,

the flowering fields,

the sight of the clouds by

day and the stars at night,

we become impoverished in

all that makes us human.

Only within the ever-renewing
processes of nature is there any
future for the human community.

Not to recognize this is to make
economics a deadly affair.

Every animal form depends ultimately on
plant forms that alone can transform the energy of
the sun and the minerals of Earth into the
living substance needed for life nourishment of
the entire animal world,
including the human community.

The well-being of the soil and the plants growing there
must be a primary concern for humans.

To disrupt this process is to break the Covenant of
the Earth and to imperil life.

We cannot have well humans on a sick planet,

not even with all our medical science.

Human health is derivative.

Planetary health is primary.

The human community and the natural world

will go into the future as a single sacred community

or we will both perish in the desert.

We have been trying to go into the future as

a human community in an exploitative relationship

with the natural community

without any sense of being integral with

this natural world as a sacred community.

From now on, that is not acceptable,

purely and simply, because it is a way not of life,

but of death.

The universe is a community of subjects,

not a collection of objects.

No matter how much these are

interrelated with each other,

if we do not hear the voices of the trees,

the birds, the animals, the fish,

the mountains and the rivers,

then we are in trouble.

I think that is one of the most

important things we are learning

from the tribal peoples of the world.

We are learning to address

the river and be addressed

by the river.

I do not mind a heaven father,

that is all right.

But I do like the idea

of an earth mother,

and I also like

to talk to the trees.

This idea that the trees talk to me

and I talk to the trees,

this kind of subjectivity,

is somehow absent

from our tradition.

A New Vision

7

Perhaps a new revelatory
experience is taking place,
an experience wherein human
consciousness awakens to the
grandeur and sacred quality of
the Earth process.

Humanity has seldom participated
in such a vision since shamanic times,
but in such a renewal lies
our hope for the future for
ourselves and for the entire planet
on which we live.

If there is to be real and sustainable progress,

it must be a continuing enhancement of life for

the entire planetary community.

It must be shared by all the living,

from the plankton in the sea to the birds above the land.

It must include the grasses, the trees,

and the living creatures of the earth.

These three commitments – to the

natural world as revelatory,

to the earth community as our primary loyalty,

and to the progress of the

community in its integrity – constitute the new

religious-spiritual context

for carrying out a change of direction

in human-earth development.

Professional education should be based on the
awareness that the earth itself is the primary physician,
primary lawgiver, primary revelation of the divine,
primary scientist, primary technologist,
primary commercial venture, primary artist,
primary educator, and primary agent
in whichever other activity we find
in human affairs.

To preserve the natural world as
the primary revelation of the
divine must be the basic
concern of religion.

We might say that we are into a phase of midwifery,

that is a phase of birthing the new structure of

the planet earth.

We ourselves need to be reborn,

the earth needs to be reborn.

We are in the process.

It is our historical role.

Our primary concern must be to
restore the organic economy of
the entire planet.

There is reason to believe that
those mysterious forces that have
guided earthly events thus far
have not suddenly collapsed
under the great volume of
human affairs.

We might think of a viable future for the planet

less as the result of some scientific insight

or as dependent on some socioeconomic arrangement

than as participation in a symphony

or as renewed presence

manifested in the wonderworld about us.

Our best procedure might be to

consider that we need not a

human answer to an earth problem,

but an earth answer to

an earth problem.

The earth will solve its problems

and possibly our own,

if we let the earth function in its own ways.

We need only listen to what

the earth is telling us.

Even beyond union with the human community

must be union with the Earth,

with the universe itself

in the full wonder of its being.

Only the Earth can adequately will the Earth.

If we will the future effectively it will be

because the guidance and the powers of the Earth

have been communicated to us,

not because we have determined the future of the Earth

simply with some rational faculty.

Our responsibility to the Earth is

not simply to preserve it,

it is to be present to the Earth

in its next sequence of transformations.

We are not lacking in the dynamic

forces needed to create the future.

We live immersed in a sea of

energy beyond all comprehension.

But this energy, in an ultimate sense,

is not ours by domination

but by invocation.

Because creatures in the universe

do not come from some place outside it,

we can only think of the universe

as a place where qualities that will

one day bloom are for the present

hidden as dimensions of emptiness.

The universe must be experienced as the Great Self.

Each is fulfilled in the other:

the Great Self is fulfilled in the individual self,

the individual self is fulfilled in

the Great Self.

In the end the universe can only be
explained in terms of celebration.
It is all an exuberant expression of
existence itself.

References

BE   Thomas Berry with Thomas Clarke
      Befriending the Earth
      Twenty-third Publications, 1991

DE   Thomas Berry
      The Dream of the Earth
      Sierra Club Books, 1990

GW   Thomas Berry
      The Great Work
      Bell Tower, 1999

US   Brian Swimme and Thomas Berry
      The Universe Story
      Harper Collins, 1992

Chapter 1: Creation's Beauty and Violence

p.17	US	p.17
p.18	US	p.17
p.19	US	p.17
p. 20	US	p.18
p.21	US	p.47
p.22	US	p.54
p.23	BE	p.19
p.24	US	p.49
p.25	US	p.51
p.26	US	p.41
p.27	US	p.56
p.28	US	p.55
p.29	US	p.60
p.30	US	p.140

Chapter 2: Diversity

p.33	US	p.74
p.34	BF	p.69
p.35	GW	p.149
p.36	DE	p.46
p.37	GW	p.26

Chapter 3: Interiority

p.41	BE	p.77
p.42	DE	p.131-132
p.43	DE	p.134
p.44	US	p.53
p.45	GW	p.25
p.46	US	p.38
p.47	US	p.41
p.48	US	p.40
p.49	US	p.40

Chapter 4: Community

p.53	BE	p.14
p.54	DE	p.91
p.55	DE	p.81
p.56	DE	p.91
p.57	BE	p.14
p.58	GW	p.147-148
p.59	US	p.77
p.60	US	p.40
p.61	BE	p.43

Chapter 5: To be Human

p.65	DE	p.132
p.66	BE	p.21
p.67	GW	p.32
p.68	BE	p.75
p.69	US	p.44
p.70	BE	p.9
p.71	GW	p.149

Chapter 6: Human Destruction

p.75	DE	p.82
p.76	DE	p.44 & p.8
p.77	BE	p.99
p.78	BE	p.20
p.79	BE	p.97
p.80	GW	p.200
p.81	BE	p.98
p.82	GW	p.200
p.83	DE	p.74-75
p.84	GW	p.148
p.85	US	p.257
p.86	BE	p.43
p.87	BE	p.43
p.88	BE	p.20
p.89	BE	p.19

Chapter 7: A New Vision

Acknowledgements

I would like to express my sincere thanks to Margaret Berry and the Thomas Berry Foundation for their permission to use Thomas Berry's work and to Brian Swimme for permission to use his.
Thanks, too, to Marty Ostrow for the lovely picture of the St Francis sculpture at the Green Mountain Monastery.
Also special thanks Stephen Wollaston for designing this book so beautifully, to Alan Shephard for the inspiration that first launched the project and above all to Marian Van Eyk McCain and my colleagues on the GreenSpirit Council for supporting me in so many ways.

~ JUNE RAYMOND

GreenSpirit Book Series & Other Resources

We hope you have enjoyed this book, and that it has whetted your appetite to read more in this series and discover the many and varied ways in which green spirituality can be expressed in every single aspect of our lives and culture.

You may also wish to visit our website, which has a members area, information about GreenSpirit's annual events, book reviews and much more: **www.greenspirit.org.uk**

*   *   *

Other titles in the GreenSpirit Book Series

What is Green Spirituality? Edited by Marian Van Eyk McCain

All Our Relations: GreenSpirit Connections with the More-than-Human World. Edited by Marian Van Eyk McCain

The Universe Story in Science and Myth. By Greg Morter and Niamh Brennan

Rivers of Green Wisdom: Exploring Christian and Yogic Earth-Centred Spirituality. By Santoshan (Stephen Wollaston)

Pathways of Green Wisdom: Discovering Earth-Centred Teachings in Spiritual and Religious Traditions. Edited by Santoshan (Stephen Wollaston)

Deep Green Living. Edited by Marian Van Eyk McCain

The Rising Water Project: Real Stories of Flooding, Real Stories of Downshifting. Compiled by Ian Mowll

Dark Nights of the Green Soul: From Darkness to New Horizons. Edited by Ian Mowll and Santoshan (Stephen Wollaston)

Awakening to Earth-Centred Consciousness: Selection from GreenSpirit magazine. Edited by Ian Mowll and Santoshan (Stephen Wollaston)

GreenSpirit Reflections. Compiled by Santoshan (Stephen Wollaston)

Anthology of Poems for GreenSpirits. Compiled by Joan Angus

The Lilypad List: Seven Stpes to the Simple Life. By Marian Van Eyk McCain

Free for
members
ebook
editions

GreenSpirit
magazine

GreenSpirit magazine is free for members and is published in both print and electronic form. Each issue includes essential topics connected with Earth-based spirituality. It honours Nature as a great teacher, celebrates the creativity and interrelatedness of all life and of the cosmos, affirms biodiversity and human differences, and honours the prophetic voice of artists.

Find out more at www.greenspirit.org.uk

For many of us, it's the spirit running through that limitless span of green organisations and ideas that anchors all the work we do. And 'GreenSpirit' is an invaluable source of insight, information and inspiration.
~ JONATHON PORRITT

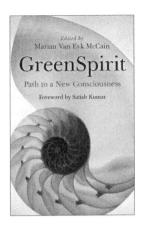

GreenSpirit
Path to a New Consciousness
Edited by Marian Van Eyk McCain

Only by understanding the Universe as a vast, holistic system and Earth as a unit within it can we help restore balance to that unit.

Only by placing Earth and its ecosystems – about which we now understand so much – at the centre of all our thinking can we avert ecological disaster.

Only by bringing our thinking back into balance with feeling, intuition and awareness and by grounding ourselves in a sense of the sacred in all things can we achieve a new level of consciousness.

Green spirituality is the key to a new, twenty-first century consciousness. And here is the most comprehensive book ever written on green spirituality.

Published by Earth Books
ISBN 978-1-84694-290-7

'*GreenSpirit: Path to a New Consciousness* offers numerous healing and inspiring insights; notably, that Earth and the universe are primary divine Revelation, a truth to be transmitted to our children as early and effectively as possible.'
~ THOMAS BERRY (January 2009)

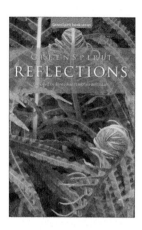

If you enjoyed *Meditations with Thomas Berry*, you might also enjoy the 10th title in our low-cost Book Series:

GreenSpirit Reflections
Compiled by Santoshan (Stephen Wollaston)

A meditations book of profound and inspiring quotations on green spirituality.

Drawing from a variety of GreenSpirit publications, this beautifully designed book of reflections gathers together numerous key insights in nine essential categories that can be seen as the core of Earth-centred wisdom: Awakening / GreenSpirit / Earth / Nature / Interconnectedness / Evolvement / Stories / The Numinous / Engagement.

The compiler, Santoshan (Stephen Wollaston), studied world religions at King's College London, is a OneSpirit Interfaith Foundation Minister, a trustee of GreenSpirit, the chair of GreenSpirit's publications committee, and an author, coauthor and editor of over a dozen books, including *Rivers of Green Wisdom: Exploring Christian and Yogic Earth-Centred Spirituality*.

118 pages
Available in hardback, paperback and various eBook formats

See GreenSpirit's Book Series webpage for more details: www.greenspirit.org.uk/books-greenspirit-book-series/

Printed in Great Britain
by Amazon